Little Pebble™

Community Helpers at a Fire

by Mari Schuh

CAPSTONE PRESS
a capstone imprint

Little Pebble is published by Capstone Press,
1710 Roe Crest Drive, North Mankato, Minnesota 56003
www.mycapstone.com

Library of Congress Cataloging-in-Publication Data
Library of Congress Cataloging-in-Publication data is on file with the Library of Congress.
ISBN 978-1-5157-2399-8 (library binding)
ISBN 978-1-5157-2409-4 (paperback)
ISBN 978-1-5157-2415-5 (ebook PDF)

Editorial Credits
Megan Atwood, editor; Juliette Peters, designer;
Pam Mitsakos, media researcher; Tori Abraham, production specialist

Photo Credits
Alamy: Fresh Start Images, 13, Maskot, 6-7; Getty Images: Comstock, 14-15, Fuse, 20-21, shaunl, 10-11; iStockphoto: MarkCoffeyPhoto, 9, Steve Debenport, 18-19; Shutterstock: Africa Studio, 16-17, bikeriderlondon, cover, Brad Sauter, 12, Mikhail Bakunovich, 3, 24, back cover, Nils Petersen, 4-5, PHOTOCREO Michal Bednarek, 21 background, S. Bonaime, 1, sandyman, 10 bottom left

Table of Contents

House Fire

A neighbor sees smoke.

A house is on fire.

Call 911!

A family runs out of the house.

They need help.

Helpers at a Fire

A fire truck rushes to the house. Firefighters make sure everyone is out. They use tall ladders.

Firefighters put out the fire.

They use long hoses.

Police officers help too.

They keep people away

from the fire.

Carlos got hurt.

A paramedic cares for him.

She takes him to the hospital.

Jill is hungry.

Volunteers give her food.

Thank you!

Jacob is cold.
An aid worker gives
him clothes.

Many people help at a fire.

These helpers save lives.

Glossary

aid worker—a person who helps people during emergencies or disasters

firefighter—a person who is trained to fight fires

neighbor—a person who lives next door or nearby

paramedic—a medical worker who takes care of hurt people during emergencies

police officer—a person who makes sure laws are being followed

volunteer—a person who does a job without being paid

Read More

Lindeen, Mary. *A Visit to the Firehouse.* A Beginning-to-Read Book. Chicago: Norwood House Press, 2016.

Ready, Dee. *Police Officers Help.* Our Community Helpers. North Mankato, Minn.: Capstone Press, 2014.

Rogers, Amy B. *What Do Firefighters Do?* Helping the Community. New York: PowerKids Press, 2016.

Internet Sites

FactHound offers a safe, fun way to find Internet sites related to this book. All of the sites on FactHound have been researched by our staff.

Here's all you do:
Visit *www.facthound.com*
Type in this code: 9781515723998

Super-cool stuff! Check out projects, games and lots more at
www.capstonekids.com

Index